Rosengarten

Rosengarten

Janice Galloway
Anne Bevan

for Isobel

with affection -

Janice
March 2004

platform projects
Hunterian Art Gallery

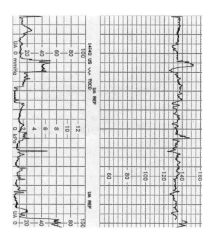

for

Celsus   that wrote describing turning in the womb

Hippocrates   that wrote the sacred oath

Vesalius   that wrote a monumental anatomy

Albuciasis   that detailed surgery

Trotula   that wrote of women

Mauriceau   that understood contractions

Levret   that systematised breech delivery

Nufer   that delivered his wife by cutting

Rösslin   that wrote the beautiful Rosengarten

Rueff   that spread the Garden wider

Paré   that advanced podalic inversion

Gallimeau   that insisted on maternal happiness

Madame de Coudray   that made a teaching machine

Récamier   that developed a speculum

Chamberlen   that concealed his forceps

Hunter   that dissected late pregnancy

Barrie   that carried the Caesarean through

Simpson   that brought the blessing of anaesthesia

Smellie   that advanced forceps

Freake   that forged forceps

Chapman   that widened the blades

Dusée   that crossed the ariculation

Holmes   that died to fight puerperal fever

Semmelweiss   that was ridiculed for washing his hands

Donald   that pictured the unborn in sound

and

all those unnamed that birthed the babies

that worked in silence

that were never book-learned

that sliced with a breadknife

that slept by the patient

that went without pay

that waited in cramped spaces

that learned by listening

that cradled the dead

that was all there was

all were there was

all there wa

wa

wa

wa

List of Contents

Foreword

Rosengarten is a collation of words, images and ideas derived from obstetric implements: the medical machinery used in difficult labours to extricate mothers from babies and, with luck, pull both through intact.

It seems almost redundant to explain why that would be interesting. Human beings are sympathetic animals. If the precision tools and skills of medicine, designed to deal near-unfathomable limits of distress, are intriguing (and they are), by rights, the tools of birthing should hold a very particular place in our empathies and our curiosity. Add to this the fact that these particular implements are in general entirely hidden from public view: covered till the last moment, most especially from those upon whom they will be immediately used, the processes of the labour room have developed a dark mystique.

Folk tales of labour itself are in no short supply: mothers, attendant fathers, midwives and doctors can each supply their own homegrown set. Some are horror stories, some comedies, some are powerfully moving: all, however, seem confined to the area of personal anecdote and are largely unrecorded as art or anything else. The implements without which these stories – and their conclusions – would largely not exist appear, if at all, as glimpses, imaginings, mere names. In some antenatal classes, discussion of obstetric contraptions is not only discouraged but also disapproved as harmful. True, one set of obstetrical implements are high-profiled in the David Cronenberg film *Dead Ringers* – but these are no more than a sinister set of fakes deliberately intended to crank up the morbid dysfunction of the film's leading men. Three hundred and forty years after the Chamberlen brothers, the first to use forceps commercially in Europe, hid their new-fangled contraption in an absurdly huge wooden chest against the prying gaze of 'outsiders', the obstetrician's armamentarium is still something of a covered box.

The implements themselves are strikingly simple. The senior obstetrician who let us see around his hospital has said as much when we confessed the focus of our research was the implements per se, rather than on the perhaps more compelling (certainly more primal) attraction of birth or of female experience. "There are only very few obstetric devices," he said, blinking as the mildly incredulous do. "And they're not very fancy." It's quite true. Those implements in commonest use are forceps and ventouse (inhalers for anaesthetic gas count at a pinch), both possessed of a frank functionality that is pleasingly counter to the euphemisms of so-called 'women's complaints'.

Raking about in the Wellcome's collections, the Edinburgh College of Surgeons' treasure trove of crates or the Hunterian Museum's glass cases, showed how little over centuries the basic designs of the implements (and the basic methodology of attendant processes) have changed while the ethics of their application – now more definitely to do with the survival of living babies and mothers than dead – has shifted dramatically. The merest glance at the histories of this development reveals daring, entrepreneurialism, mental toughness (the demands of complex labours requiring surgery in a time before anaesthesia beggar belief) and tempering compassion.

Of course, conception and contraception and the devices they have attracted over millennia were impossible to ignore, as were the connections between them. A sidelong look at processes such as Caesarean section seemed apt. Further connections (between magic and technology; between the church and centuries of taken-for-granted suffering; between teaching texts and courage and philanthropy; between the man-made and the human hands that were the labouring woman's only source of comfort for centuries) we made as we went along. Water, garden plants, the textures of natural materials (rubber, metal, glass, silk) inform the words, the sculptures and the pictures: a suggestion of things visible, fluid, cast with light.

Away from the heat and trauma of birth, seen in isolation or reflection, the implements, the processes which surround them, made to fit the curves and lines of female interiors, to clasp the most vulnerable of human beings, became beautiful, not only in design but in intention. We hope a little of that beauty showa in the words and pictures in this book.

The name of this book comes from Eucharius Rösslin's *Der Swangern Frauwen und Hebammen Rosengarten* (1513), the first illustrated manual of midwifery. Rösslin took the opportunity given by the advent of the new printing press to publish in German so midwives, unversed in Latin, might read it or, as the book advises, have it read to them by 'a well-read woman'. Jacob Rueff's updated, enlarged and improved 1587 edition added detailed information on conception, generation, birthing techniques and ethics. Jost Amman's magnificent woodcuts include illustrations of the positions of the foetus in utero, Adam and Eve and, most delightfully of all, a scene of a woman on a birth-stool flanked by female attendants as the midwife performs her duties. Implements are in a bag fastened to the midwife's belt, scissors and twine for the umbilical cord may be seen on a bank of pillows, astrologers gaze up at stars and a bath waits off-centre for the soon-to-come child.

The book's title means, of course, The Rose Garden.

Janice Galloway

seed

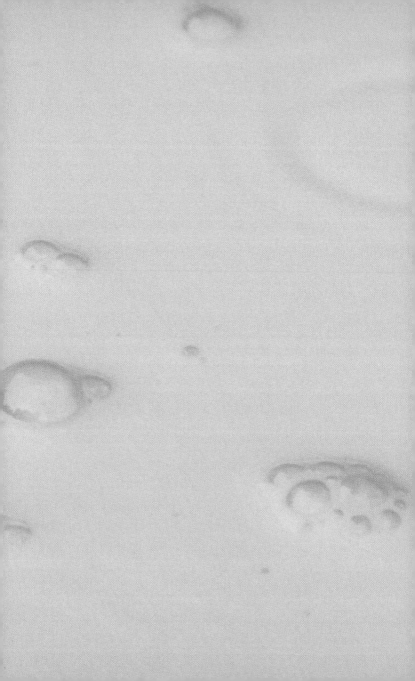

There are arguments of the church and the arguments of philosophy. The arguments of the body. Of desire.

No contest.

Sap rises. It's what it does. We're only human.

There's no forgetting circuitry: these tendrils snubbing tips through solid stone.

Our deviousness. Our succulence.

Our squirming, feral hearts.

To be or not to be.
It's always been a question.

The need to stopper that most natural of conclusions, to con
conception, is surely old enough, practiced enough (whatever
clergy say) to count as natural.

Consider then the implements, the range of what is needed.

> Take the testicles of a weasel and wrap them up,
> binding them to the thigh of a woman who also
> wears a weasel bone on her person and she will
> no longer conceive.

There are fumigations, douches, soaks and grains
to clog the uteris, or simply slick a promise safe.

a clot of dung or honey, viscous, slick as resin
earwax of a dray or cedar
oil, acacia, alcohol, acids of all stripes or
pomegranate halves and lavender

a clock

Perhaps a bag, a convex rubber mouth

a wrap of lamb's intestine liberally applied
a hollowed bowl of rubber,
lemon, pea-pod shells, a sliver
latex-skin that's acrid to the tongue

will do the trick. Or maybe won't.

Stand, jump: DO NOT SIT STILL.
Do not become a pit, a well, a sponge.

Measure time and temperatures, gauge weights.

a clock
a calendar
a clock

How many jars and coptics, spells
Queen Anne's Lace
mustard seed and silver mercury
a deadening dose of lead
and letters (Dutch or French) we'll try;
how many barbed and dry yet deftly-made inventions,
if the sheets are waiting, keen.

Here come a coil of IUDs.

A Lippes Loop, a Russian Twist
An Omega,
An Anchor.
The Antigon, an Ypsilon,
the Grafenberg and Gynae T and Scoy and Golden Lily,
the CU Safe and Inhiband,
the Comet and a Dalcon Shield, Duck's Foot, Bull's Head and
Butterfly, the Shambrock (Irish, disallowed) and
May Zhin Spring to keep us out of scrapes.

they're fishhooks
lint and bandage, copper, cobalt,
platinum, gold

Some look like ariels, aliens.
All are wishbones, broken. Whale-jaw split in two.

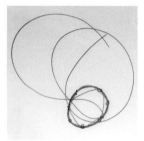

And in extremis, out of doors, caught short, perhaps
mere anything will do. An amulet,
a thermos lid, a wrapper, strips of cooking film,
a sneeze, a wing, a prayer.

This is the force of need, of foolishness, of thrall to now. To this.
Then when you are braced, whether you are braced, concede.

Conceive.

Admit it.

Fall.

plant

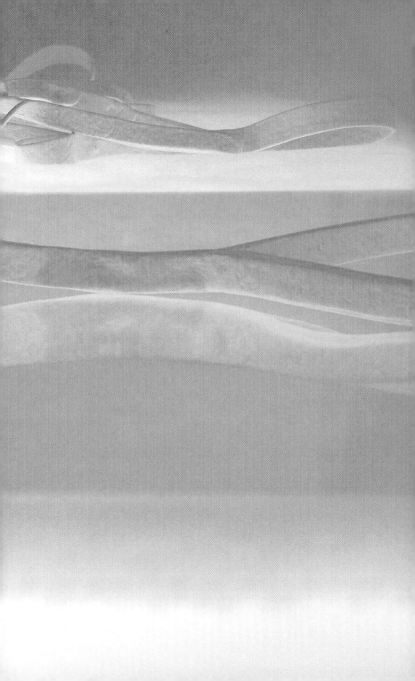

Fall.
It's the verb we use of pregnancy, of love.
In or out. Either way. One falls.

A wish, a gooseberry bush.
A spill of milk.

Some, however, need a shove:
a bringing on or setting off, some light induction.

Any childless woman of forty will tell you.
That thought, that shift of emphasis occurs.

Take dates and raisins, nutmeg, clove and catmint
and heat them through. Add a syrop next of orris
root and ox-tail brotha tilted bed, the scents of
rose and jasmine and any warming spice. She will
fall in two days.

And if at first you don't conceive, try, try again.

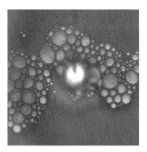

Method:

Find pipes and tubes a
fine pipette and a flat, glass base
a needle with a hollow core
the rapid movement of the solitary hand

(thermometer, a calendar, a clock
a clock
the body's treacherous heat)

and wait
and wait

and wait.

Weigh, test, measure. As you will.
Nothing's certain till it is.

Let those who will, last the course and fall at the appropriate
hurdle. The last, of course.

The last.

From missing blood to broken bag of brine
a needle on a thread, translucent jelly,
a picture made of bounces sparkling on a screen
the eye, a jug
a die, a mould, is cast.

Then bide its time. A pregnancy is patience, nothing but.

Condense and thicken.

Do not drink. Thrive.

This is the business of life with death, the two in precise relation. This is the business of drawing air and of drowning fluids, of slickness and dry compression. The business of making two from one, connecting nerves and channels and down and muscle, veins. Dark to light, a business carried out under the broil of woollen covers, a business of touch and steel and random happenstance.

There is bleeding of course. And splitting and surrender. All quite beyond control.

But come when you are called. Attend: this most of all.
Be a midwife if you cannot be a mother.

Offer drinks from a narrow straw. Make calm, speak soft. Close the windows tight to keep the uninvited from entering. Stoke a fire to its fullest, set a child to tend the coals for luck. Make ready oils and plasters, poultice, fumigations, gall and bitter herbs, cloths and holy water, good victuals, ale, the implements and dials, probes and lances, wires, curve-handled shafts. And mark the clock, the moon.

Call an astrologer to begin the ephemeris.

Flex your fingers.

Crack your knuckles.

Wash your hands.

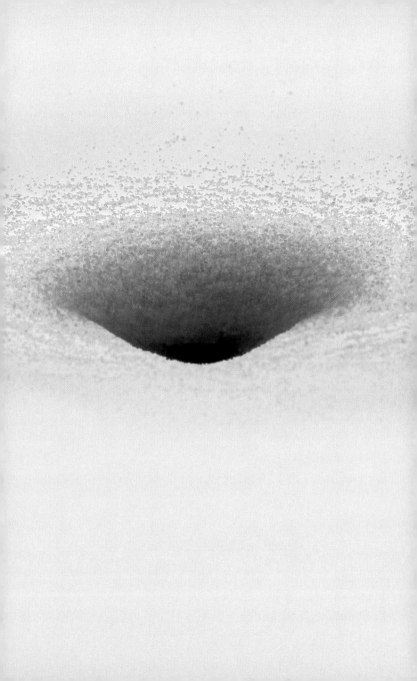

inner

space

outer

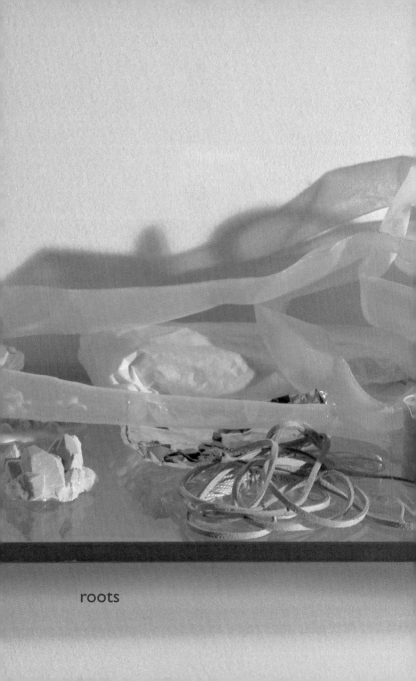

roots

Trotula of Salerno

Lowering the Price of Fruit in a Fixed Market

Fallen as an apple, her white skin bruised, Eve incurred a price.
Her anatomy, they said, was shameful now; her pain, God-given.

For centuries, the church and all admitted practise made it
true. The medicine of the Romans, their birthing chairs and
Hippocratic cant were lost. No laying on of hands, no cries for help,
no interference. Birth in sorrow, that'll teach you. Relief be damned.

What midwives did in secret, they did in secret. Few read.
There was nothing to read in any case, not on this subject.
Many guessed. Some carried whips the better to sharpen the
punishment already on its way. Some turned up drunk and few
complained. Some worked and wept and managed little miracles
nonetheless. All lap of the gods, you might say: all luck of the bloody,
loaded draw.

The School of Salerno, no-one knows when, began a difference.
This eleventh century hospital, teaching while King Harold lost his
eye, while the Normans obsessed about their boundaries, taught
medicine by the shores of the Tyrrhenian Sea. Its land was Sicilian,
its language, Greek. It was the finest teaching school in Europe and
Trotula, specialist in falling sickness, dropsy and diseases of the skin,
in female anatomy and pregnancy and birth, was its finest teacher.
It was possible, she opined, that one might offer gentleness to the
suffering in labour. It was possible she insisted, to use the skill of

medicine to assist. What's more she wrote it down: all sixty three chapters of obstetric, gynaecological and dietary advice, all female. Trust and touch, she said. Ask questions of the sick. Believe your ears. Her meaning was embroidered there for even priests to see. For suffering alone is nothing godly. *Administer hemlock, hyocyanus, a soothing oil*. For we must refuse the price. Offer all assistance possible, for pity's sake, for the sake of God. For shame. For shame.

Doctor Wertt

Knowledge

Consider knowledge. What it might be, its uses, its fearful dangers.
Consider Dr Wertt.

They had lost the skills of the Romans. Of Soranus and the
obstetric chair. The midwife, one who knew from what she saw,
was whom they turned to, if they turned at all. Her bottle of ale,
some coin for her troubles: they'll give her she was cheap. She had
her herbs, her prayers, her amulets, the cat to keep from the
afterbirth. Occasionally, a knife, a whip. She moved singly, kept her
counsel. The church kept her straight.

Dr Wertt was marked for medicine from birth by the
insertionary slenderness of his fingers, the burning curiosity of
his gaze. By the age of five, he possessed his own flaying knife,
opened rats, domestic kittens and rabbits if he found them. He
kept leeches in a jar. At six, he saw his mother fall into a swound
and seep, melting over the floor. Thereafter, some terrible business
behind the locked doors of his mother's rooms left him alone with
his father, who was too distracted to care that he cried. The tiny,
swaddled corpse he was shown afterwards was no compensation.
He never forgot.

At thirteen, he entered the university to be versed in Medicine
and natural law, Latin and mathematics. He won prizes for his
Greek, that most cursive of languages rendered cleaner by the
jagged arches of his German hand. By seventeen, he could sew

together a leg or hand that had been mangled by a cheese press, piece back the bones of a face or foot, mend slashes, drill-holes and seeping sores. He might mash, boil and distil his own medicines and bleed, purge, drain, cauterise, amputate and even trepan if need arose. He could mend the pox with subtle applications of wasp stings and filtered red light. Still he knew as little more of the processes of birthing than any clod keeping cows in an open field.

True, he knew what the swollen belly meant and how its various shapes might be interpreted; that a greater angle of incline of the flesh to the fore meant a male child, that wider girth most likely presaged a girl. But by state and church law, he might not enter a room with a labouring female. Only midwives might. Midwives who were not book-read, who lived with goats and chickens for company, who ead no Greek. Though at times, to comfort himself, he chose to think that whatever midwives had amounted to nothing much, he wished he had it too. He wished to watch as the glory of life unfolded, literally, in a red swathe before his eyes. He wished to see and place his hands upon a newborn warm from the womb, scarlet as a flayed hide. Dr Wertt suspected that beyond the strips of linen soaked in lavender water, more still than the oils they slathered over the waiting mother's flesh, these women with their ale bottles and bunches of raspberry leaves at their belts, used some kind of device that he, a doctor, might not demand to see. And he resented it. He resented it a great deal.

His curiosity burning like eczema, his imaginings lurid enough to disturb his sleep, Dr Wertt, could finally contain himself no longer. Perhaps following goading from his fellows, perhaps in his cups, perhaps because the birth to be was in rooms next to his own and the opportunity seemed too good to ignore, Dr Wertt did something he should not. He did something against all the strictures of the church, the times, the civil and moral laws of Hamburg. He shaved his still-boyish face clean as he could manage, pinched his cheeks and bit his lips and dressed as someone else. A maid's overdress, a plain linen shirt with its sleeves ravelled to the wrists, a clean, drab apron and pattens made the beginnings of his transformation: the pale, course wimple and veil made it complete. Almost. He bided his time, near feverish with the plot; he picked the moment (a midwife called for, his own hooded self waiting at the requisite door when she arrived, unquestioning of his assistance as merely family help); he attained the room and beheld for himself a woman in fine distress, her child already fighting his way to the shuttered, secret air. If it had not been for his inability to take the orders of the midwife, his soft and white-nailed hands, he might well have succeeded. As it was, almost too late, the midwife asked and outright. A dress, she said afterwards, giving testimony as best she could. A man in the chamber was devilish enough, but *in a dress*. She blushed, let her fingers bubble on the seam of her rosary. *A dress*.

They tried him in hose and doublet, a cod-piece big enough to front a ship. Even so, he was judged to the full letter of theological law. Whatever his training, his promise, his use, he had thrown it away in one rash act, in his wish to know too much. And this despite his birth, his blood. His nobler sex. What choice remained? He'd burn for sure, learn the hard way. He'd certainly burn.

Students might have made of it an empirical test: examined the effect of naked flame on naked aspiration; on the skin, the lungs, on massy, reaming flesh. Doubtless they did not.

And the price of knowledge is that it must be won again, again. By inches, degrees. One may die for it, or from lack of it. Choose.

Choose wisely. Think what has been gained before, its cost, its prize. Remember Dr Wertt.

Forceps

Obstetric forceps have a long a history, but their beginnings, in classical Greece, saw their use as solely destructive. Early forceps, in conjunction with a knitting-needle device called a crotchet, was used expressly to crush the foetal skull the faster to void the foetus in a last-ditch attempt to save a mother's life. It's certain that severe physical (and doubtless mental) consequences would have resulted, that is, if the woman survived at all. Only much later did the possibility of using these metal arms to hold an infant with the purpose of assisting live birth occur.

They are generally agreed to have been the secret of the William Chamberlen family from around 1650. The Chamberlens concealed their 'machine' for many years, arriving in birthing chambers with a huge box carried by two men – a deliberate tactic to avoid even the remotest conjecture, even by the patient, as to what lay within. Perpetration of this subterfuge was easily possible because religion's induction of shame regarding women's genitalia meant most obstetric procedures were carried out under layers of sheeting. Not till 1700 did the Chamberlen forceps come to light, the instruments thereafter acquiring such cachet, they were common in European cities by 1733.

While these saved the lives of some babies who would otherwise have been removed piecemeal from the womb, the 'high forceps' of the eighteenth century could inflict ferocious levels of foetal damage, infection, and lifelong lacerations of the vagina and perineum to the woman who endured their use. Even so, forceps were an incalculable advance in the treatment of obstructed labour – a genuine alternative offering life rather than death by eventual, grudging Caesarean section or exhaustion. Since forceps were an implement costing a good deal and demanding training in their use, it could be said that their restricted use began a potentially damaging split between midwifery (almost wholly the province of women and low-paid) and obstetrical doctoring (the opposite) that can still cause argument today.

William Smellie, a family GP from Lanark, studied obstetrics in Paris, thereafter setting up a midwifery school off Pall Mall in London, charging a fee of five shillings for his lessons. Smellie's finest achievement was in altering the design of forceps (wood or steel padded with leather, a simple lock and short arms, for use only after the baby's head had entered the pelvis) and their application (he was one of the first to realise that the foetal head rotated during labour, his teaching of this basic fact saving foetal damage and therefore, lives). He was also the first to revive babies who were not breathing by the use of a silver catheter to inflate their lungs.

Forceps today are made of steel with two moveable arms (blades) which lock and unlock to obtain the right grip, their curves are designed to slide, with considerable manual persuasion, into the mother's vagina when sufficiently lubricated, then to clamp the baby's head as securely but comfortably as possible, given the circumstances. They are probably the best-known of all obstetrical implements, by name if nothing else. High Forceps, which caused so much dread in the nineteenth century, are no longer used.

There are different kinds of forceps because every baby, every mother, is different.

We are, however, alike enough for these instruments to be generally similar, and to work in much the same way: to offer, if used correctly, a hopeful, breathing, chance.

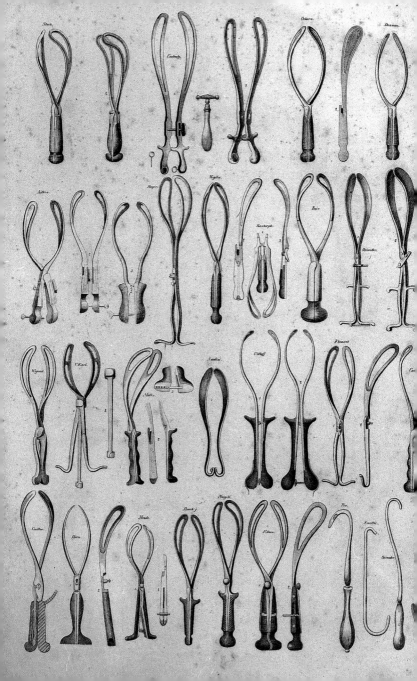

TAB. XXXV.

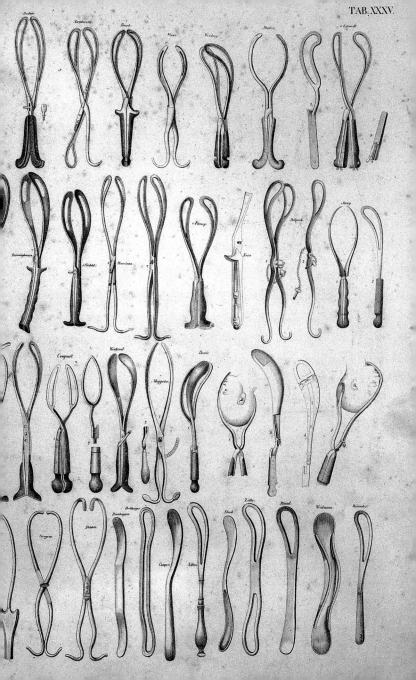

Chamberlen, Dusée, Smellie

The Hands of God

Chamberlen conceived and concealed them,
Dusée articulated them,
Smellie fitted an assemblage, a battery, a
Tour de force of locks.

Van Deventer, Hunter, a score of Lancet letterists
thought them callous to immodest, though certainly
true to God himself, these claws increased Eve's pains.
Expensive, tooled, engraved, the doctor's status symbols
Hung like keys about his belt.

No matter. In whatever form
(hinged, short or long, articulated,
covered, naked, greased) these
salad leaves of ironmongery survived.

Survive.

Three hundred years of forceps in museum rows:
slingbacks in Imelda Marcos closets, lie resting from their labours,
waiting for something to savour, something to save, one
final, crimson, call.

Marguerite de Coudray

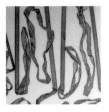

La Machine, le corps, le mot

Marguerite du Coudray, matron of Rouen, the city that burned at stake the living Jeanne d'Arc, wished to teach the midwives of France. Thus she thought they might more humanely assist the newborn citizen to a foothold in the shifting world. A machine and a book: one taught by ink the other by example. Both.

Law and church did not mind a lack of learning, indeed, they fostered it. Midwives must attest their virtue, of course; they must be passed as wholesome by a priest, free of the taint of witchcraft or the desire to obtain power. But study? Jesu, no. Still, Marguerite du Coudray, her manikin, her baby dolls of darkest pink, her dyed-string umbilicals and porous sponge placentas bouncing on the carriage seat beside her, travelled through revolution and clergy, through every sort of weather, through thirty years of guillotines, slicing. Heedless. Not, however, headless, despite the odds.

The body of woman, the machine. Example following precept. *I bring you names, show you the pieces to which they accrue.*

Naming is power, force, the beginning of everything.
She carried the word, hidden in a placket pocket.

The word. The word.

ink

water

blood

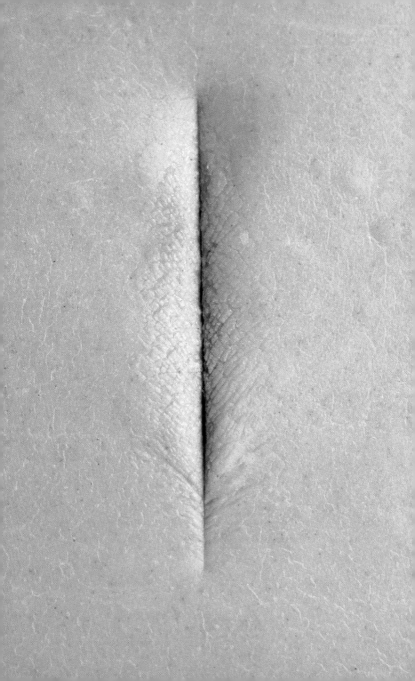

Ceasarean Section

Caesarean section seems to have been in recorded use since 700 AD. Since Roman law declared that dead pregnant women could not be buried without the foetus having been removed, the whole procedure was post mortem and for legal, not medical, reasons. The term, from the Latin caedare, 'to cut' has nothing to do with Julius or any other caesar, despite persistent folklore. Under Christian sway, Europe turned away from Roman knowledge, and Caesarean section did not reappear till the 1460's, as a procedure carried out on women who had died or were dying in childbirth to try and save the infant. One (almost certainly false) tale from 1500 claims Jacob Nufer, a vet from Switzerland, delivered his own child after thirteen midwives had given up, and that both mother and child lived.

In medieval times, Caesarean section (which is, of course, invasive surgery) was only extremely infrequently performed on live mothers. Since the operation meant cutting into the abdomen, pushing the intestines aside then cutting into the uteris to create a wound that would probably not heal, and this on a fully conscious patient, it is unsurprising. Jean Ruleau's successful operation of 1689 is often regarded as the first European attempt in which both mother and child survived. By the end of the eighteenth century, caesareans had a success rate of around 25 per cent. The alternative was to dissect the baby in utero and remove it in the hope of saving the mother. Neither option was pleasant. Even after the advent of forceps, especially if the baby was trapped high in the pelvis, section was probably the only hope.

Though women, barred from eighteenth and nineteenth century medical schools, were likewise debarred from performing Caesareans, a female midwife reported a successful Caesarean, the first operation of this kind in Britain, in 1738. She remains nameless, however, and there is no documentary evidence (necessarily supplied by a male surgeon) of support. Another woman (some argue a hermaphrodite) performed the first successful section in the British Empire. James Miranda Barrie, whose original identity remains a matter of intense speculation, trained as a surgeon at Edinburgh University disguised as a young man. After years of successful gender deception and a distinguished army medical career, he/she carried out the procedure on a Mrs Munnick whilst serving as British Army Physician at the Cape on 25th July 1826. It was not until common use of anaesthesia, antisepsis, and asepsis, however, that Ceasarean emerged as a less desperate procedure, its case strengthened by the invention of silver sutures for wounds.

It may now be reasonably argued that the incidence of Caesarean births are unnecessarily high. Trends in the USA indicate that voluntary Caesarean section rates average almost 25 per cent of all births – the former survival rate of the tiny number of mothers forced by circumstances to undergo the operation two centuries ago – largely for reasons other than the strictly medical. Ignorance of history has perhaps made us casual, demanding. Patients nowadays can confidently expect both mother and child to survive, which is a blessing. They usually do – which is another. Ceasarean section is still, of course, invasive surgery.

James Miranda Barrie

A Covered Wound

He was not the first. Neither was she. This slicing operation had a history: bloody, swift, cold.

Wilhelmina Munnick, though, was suffering. Thomas Munnick too. He called the doctor knowing what it meant. He called the best. He called in Barrie.

He'd studied hernia, this little man, in Edinburgh. Trained with Hamilton and Young in gynaecology and lying-in, he knew the latest thing. He'd plumbed the mysteries of the urogenital systems of both male and female and the diseases thereof, had delved whole-sale into syphilis and ghonorrhoea and persons of indeterminate gender, indeterminate place (for reasons, doubtless, of his own). For all his stuffy, stuffed red jacket and his military hat, he'd shown compassion for people stateless, friendless: the mad, those eaten up with leprosy, the enslaved.

But this, this plunder of soft tissue in the cot before him, this, despite the chaos, was not madness or disease. Or lovelessness. Or sex come to that.

Come to this, it was a kitchen table, knives and kidney bowls. It was gauze, a compress, plastered straps, the memory of dissection. A clock. A deal of lint and laundered cloth. And raging nerve.

The effrontery is what strikes.

His golden epaulettes, his slight-shouldered jacket, draped on the chairback, flaring. His collar tight to hide the bandage round his chest. The casual roll of his shirtsleeves, his slender wrists, his own wound no-one's business but his own.

It came to this: his red hands, her hands, working.

Chloroform and Ether

At the first winter meeting of the Medico-Chirurgical Society of Edinburgh, held on the 10th of November last (which is to say 1846), I had an opportunity of directing the attention of the members to a new agent which I had been using for some time previously, for the purpose of producing insensibility to pain in surgical and obstetric practice. This new anæsthetic agent is chloroform, chloroformyle, or perchloride of formyle. Its composition is expressed by the chemical formula $C2HCl3$. It can be procured by various processes, as by making milk of lime, or an aqueous solution of caustic alkali, act upon chloral; by distilling alcohol, pyroxylic spirit, or acetone, with chloride of lime; by leading a stream of chlorine gas into a solution of cuastic potass, in spirit of wine, &c. The resulting chloroform obtained by these processes is a heavy, clear, transparent liquid, with a specific gravity as high as 1.480. It is not inflammable. It evaporates readily, and boils at 140°. It possesses an agreeable, fragrant, fruit-like odour, and a saccharine, pleasant taste.

James Young Simpson, the son of a baker, was born in 1811 at Bathgate, Linlithgowshire and studied midwifery in Edinburgh. He was profoundly struck during his training by the horror and extent of human suffering in the operating theatre, repeating that when he saw the pain and fear endured by an elderly Highlander undergoing radical mastectomy in his lecture hall, he immediately vowed to be a bank teller instead.

Without much in the way of explanation to the patient save strong men to hold him or her down (four were the usual number), surgical practise was certainly a form of torture. Alcohol and/or the speed with which a surgeon could wield the scalpel were the only pain-relief methods that might be employed. Simpson's wish to alleviate suffering was general, but his specialism was obstetrics, and he was a passionate advocate for the needs of pregnant women. He furthered the cautious use of forceps and wrote many papers on humane treatment in difficult labours. He is probably best known, however, for his experiments with chloroform. After the gas had been successfully used by an American dentist to remove a patient's facial tumour, his studies became avid. He tested chloroform upon himself and other family members, frequently rendering them insensible at the dinner table once the plates had been cleared. In 1847, he was confident enough to try his chloroform inhaler on a female patient expecting her second child with conclusively positive results. He experienced enormous opposition, however, from those who still insisted that to lessen pain, particularly the pain and mortal danger of childbirth, was against God's wishes. In 1853 Queen Victoria, as Defender of the Faith, removed the thunder from religious argument by using chloroform herself during the birth of her eighth and ninth children. The queen gave Simpson a baronetcy in 1866.

His finest hour, however, must have been in his first successful trials of general anaesthesia, without which modern surgery could not have advanced. Without which, indeed, it would be unthinkable.

Simpson the Obstetrician

The Birth of Saint Anaesthesia

On walks across the Meadows, it was commonly observed Simpson talked to himself, seemed oblivious to his surroundings. Patients, their shuddering bellies before them, sat all day on his fine staircase so his wife could not obtain ready access to their upstairs rooms: a spur, he claimed, a reminder. This was his work.

Every morning members of the faculty called at the house to see if he was conscious. In general he was, and ready to progress. The moment found itself; the right patient, likewise. Her last confinement – three days of howling, scars and a dead infant to show – had rendered her terrified of and for what she carried. Her pains were sharp as the Edinburgh haar. Yes, she agreed. He might do as he wished. And soon. Soon. When she woke, less than two hours later, she seemed embarrassed, confused. Nothing could have prepared her for the shock of the live child, her own lack of stitching, her own body still much as it had been before. Still whole. With effort, the obstetrician persuade her to accept her baby from his arms, to embrace it.

To open her hands. To receive.

Queen Victoria

The Falling-off of Eve

There was chloroform, there was pain and she was the Queen of England, Defender of the Faith, supreme head of the church and Mother of the British Empire. There was no conundrum, theological or medical. There were only Leopold and Beatrice, drowsy but hale.

She recalled the gas tube, her knuckles white, refusing to let go, the spangled, floating room. Her husband, they say, was all approval. How he smiled.

Time Eve had her pardon. Let it go.

Let it go.

Vacuum Extraction or Ventouse

Cupping to clean and clear wounds of blood or obnoxious fluids is a very old practise, common enough in medieval Europe to be regarded as routine. A cup, often of heated glass, was placed around a wound to 'suck' the wound in the hope of healing. A version of this technique to assist vaginal delivery exists from 1705: a 'warmed glass cup' attached to the foetal cranium, by dint of the vacuum created, to draw the child down the birth canal. The danger of drawing in vaginal tissue from the mother was a constant and extremely dangerous hazard, however. and only 100 years later did a safer version, devised by Edinburgh obstetrician, James Young Simpson, arrive. Already well-kent for advocacy of chloroform, Simpson was first recorded using his own Vacuum Extraction Device in 1849. His bell-shaped 'air tractor vacuum extractor' was effective but strongly opposed as 'unnatural' and he gave up further development.

It was not until the 1950s that Malmström, a Scandinavian doctor, created the stainless steel cup instrument that is the basis of what is used today. This extractor had a mushroom-shaped cup varying from 40 to 60 mm in diameter, with a centrally attached chain connecting the cup to the traction handle.

The device used now is of soft, moulded rubber and still noticeably vacuum-cleaner-ish in look. Soft-cup extractors have an attached pump to provide the traction and no handle. They cause fewer neo-natal scalp injuries, but have a higher failure rate than their metal-cup predecessors.

A baby birthed with the aid of a ventouse will have a bump on his or her head, where the suction cup drew into itself the still-soft skull-tip. Mothers will certainly require an episiotomy (a cutting of the flesh between vagina and anus) to allow the ventouse to be inserted. Metal forceps are still, however, more commonly used to assist complicated births.

Simpson and Malmström

The Vacuum Cure

The ancients knew the score.
Metal or glass, a mouth closed firm around a wound was just the
simplest way to draw its juice.

Pus, blood and humours all responded to its kiss: why not a child?

Apply a cup, the unborn infant skull being still
as flexible as peel, and let mere nothing, *nada*, void
begin its work.

If the skin does not catch, the lining holds
then inch by sticky inch the stubborn babe slicks clean.

He that once would crush to eggshell
comes a prince again, a hero, a survivor, crowned.

Ian Donald

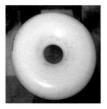

Ultrasound

Where it comes from is no-one's guess.
We know. From wartime sonar, radar
dolphins crying in the open sea.

The act of imagination, placing submarines below the skin
to track and trace their journey.
20,000 pulses drill each second, reaching
down through muscle mass
though tissue, bone.
This shattered shape in space
a firework show
is something yet to be.

Look, tracking the scanner back and back again
(a dog whistle in an echo chamber,
a mirror map): they read so easily, revealing
plain by purl
a ball of human knitting.

Unfathomable. A future through a spyglass.
Look. See its hooded eyes
its hands like fish.

bloom

Undercover till the last, we hear and sense them.
Imagine them by feel.

glass	gas	flesh
thread	water	rubber
steel	tube	ink

air	stirrup	sponge
filter	hose	silver
blood	vaseline	saline

needle	hook	plastic
cotton	blade	fibre
ice	hand	breath

Theatre (1)

nothing here is new

the crack-backed cough of laundry
cold as morning floods
the window glass

and overhead these
bandaged rubber tubes
this white-hot light

the birth room smells of paper
gag-dry cotton
burning paint

a stitch, a hook
these clocks still marking time

the door an open slice
but there's no running now.

lie back then on its folds assume
this ancient, howling space

the birthing room, resonant with cloches
clattering with spears
the silence of anaemone fronds

where no thing
every thing is

new

Theatre (2)

Pallid pinks and blues, this neutralised aqua, certainly.
This mummy paper covers most that's
sharp or stainless,
hooked or barbed or edged in crepe-white
parcels, its zebra-tape at
almost
jaunty
angles. Look this

snakery of hoses shows in
buttercup and scarlet, mauve a
wave of rubber-blue.
There are
fifteen clocks and faces
(numbered, count them) a
battery of surveillance dials, chrome.

There are no minutes more.

Someone takes the handles, shifts the mouse-squeak wheels.
And what is not blur and bumping is the
the jolt of this metal mattress,
the moonfaced bee-hive pyre of light
the feeling, overwhelming, of now.

Flat on your back, catch the blur of blue-wrapped feet,
a stranger stripping needles.

Someone has marked an armband,
permanent, in red. It says

your name.

Caesarean

The softest and most vulnerable of sites
lies open on the table. Ready, almost, to eat.

Here are
red and silver,
black lines in jagged machine-hand
a heart-line on the monitor. Its flashing separator
makes a morning alarm,
lurid
set to go.

The cover where the wound will be shows
green as mould.

Look down. See these scissors in the grass
a razor,
strops,
the gardener masking pallid thumbs.

The Shears, the Roses

a silky ladder
a lifting sling
a listening trumpet

bold striped straws
stirrups
hooks   eyes

scissors, scalpels, flensing knives
gauze and cotton
kidney bowls   and
gloves

syringes   needles
threads of course these
coloured threads

then forceps (short)
a hoover for the corners
(skull and crossblades) and
these gentle hands, these tight-trimmed nails
that know the drill quite blind

for thirsty work (and cutting if it comes to that)
these goggles, masks
plain cutlery set neat upon a tray

some prune, some scythe
some merely notch or slip between
some hollow, dig or cleave or stitch
some bind, some tie and splint
all strive

if flesh tears (and it does)
then let it tear.
it weeps while muscles shudder to the task
we are and aren't as fragile as you'd think

for this (and more than all of this) these
gardeners assembled here,
these midwives, obstetricians, handlers,
ministers to human pain or joy,
these hoes and splints
are here for you

and after
when the shouting's done
these weapons, these mechanics stitch
you whole again together

if they can

if

they can

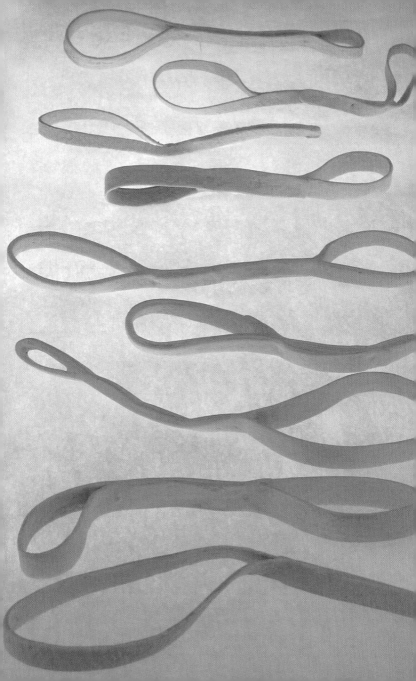

Morning Tray

Afterward, she thought they resembled
vegetables.
Fronds or greenery, loop-shaped
first leaves unstoppable
against gravity
through frozen ground.

She recalls the sear of frost,
these heathen blades
as hard as harrows
separate as bone.

The white coat is disappearing, ghosts fading out. They all look like mechanics: those mask mouths, those price-appraising eyes.

LIFE ♥ TRACE®

FSE 2050
Fetal Spiral Electrode

REF
Reorder/Part No.
31019436

+H593310194360G

STERILE R

Single Helix   Contents of unopened and   Single Use Only
                  undamaged package are sterile

Some hate all this. Not me. I have a life: it's pulsing. There's it goes, slithering from my shoulder in a wet, warm tube, gurgling under skin-pink tape. They know me, sit restless with their hands outstretched to catch me on a bed of flesh. I am wanted, prayed for. This watchfulness of plastic, metal, sticky bands, these clocks along the walls tick to my tune. Lifetimes of learning, suffering, taking stock and leaps of faith are on my side. The dead have done their bit. They're praying for me. Let the living sweat and wait. Out there is light and gas and air, a warm-lined box, a gel-filled ocean. They can see my picture sparkle on a screen, can read my thoughts. Between two worlds, I suck my thumb, sit tight. My feet, pressed on these slippy walls, feel tremors, sparks of warning, something beating, dark.

DIRECTIONS FOR USE

Remove from package and release the wires from between the Drive and Guide Tubes. Do not release wires from Handle Notch at this time. The Safety Tab should remain tucked into the Guide Tube, holding the Spiral Electrode retracted.

1. With the patient in the dorsal lithotomy position, perform a vaginal examination and identify the fetal presenting part.

2. Place the Guide Tube firmly against the identified fetal presenting part.

3. To release the Safety Tab, gently pull the Drive Handle back slightly (1 cm), then advance the Drive Rod until the Spiral Electrode touches the fetal presenting part.

4. Maintain pressure against the fetal presenting part with Guide Tube and Drive Rod. Turn the Drive Rod by rotating the Drive Handle clockwise until gentle resistance is encountered. Resistance to further rotation and recoil of the Drive Handle indicates attachment. This will usually occur after one complete rotation.

5. Release the wires from the Handle Notch. Slide the Drive and Guide Tubes off the Electrode Wires.

6. Attach the (color coded) spiral electrode wires to the appropriate terminals on the leg plate.

To detach the Spiral Electrode, rotate Spiral Electrode counter-clockwise until it is free from the fetal presenting part. Do not pull the electrode from the fetal skin.

Leaves, Off-shoots & Notes

Glossary

Caesarean section – a surgical procedure where an incision is made through the mother's abdomen and into the uteris. Caesarean operations can be carried put for reasons such as maternal diabetes, or because complications arise during normal labour, e.g. breech (bottom first rather than head-first) birth or placenta praevia (the placenta being in too low a position). For centuries, this was always a fatal operation and, until the introduction of anaesthesia, dreaded even when not. Now, some women are confident enough of modern surgical techniques to choose Caesarean almost as if it were an alternative method of delivery rather than an emergency procedure, a trend which concerns many in the medical profession as it is more dangerous on several counts than normal vaginal delivery. Caesarean procedures are usually carried out under general anaesthetic, though some women opt for an epidural (where anaesthetic is inserted into the pelvic area) and remain awake throughout the process. Vaginal delivery is entirely feasible for subsequent pregnancies.

Cervical Cap or diaphragm – device fitted (or stuck) over the neck of the cervix to prevent the entry of semen and therefore prevent pregnancy. Early versions included clods of crocodile and elephant dung (ancient Egyptian), or tampons soaked in honey, gums or aromatic oils. A squeezed half-lemon was recommended by Casanova in the 1650s. Rubber, latex chrome, plastic and silver have been used extensively in more modern times.

Condom – device worn most often by men (a female version does exist but is much less popular) to prevent pregnancy by catching semen before it enters the vagina, an idea dating from the early 1600s. They were originally made of sheep's intestine (caecum) since it was flexible and pleasingly thin. Mass production of condoms began in 1844 when Goodyear patented the vulcanisation of rubber. Makeshift or improvised condoms used in extremis include cling-wrap and sweet wrappers (a Crunchie wrapper is a reputed favourite).

Cotton swabs – in a vacuum pack to preserve their sterility.

Cotton wadding – for mopping up fluid spills.

Dilators – devices which help expand the birth canal or help reconstruct it after a damaging labour: made of glass with an indent for the thumb for easy extraction.

Fillets (also known as Chamberlen's silk fillets, loops or lacs) – Smooth tapes, probably the first devices used to assist delivery with minimal trauma and possibility of saving the child. Used since time of Hippocrates, originally made of cotton, silk or leather, then later of cane, whalebone, horsehair, wire or steel strips (the latter usually in wood or metal mounts). It was claimed that fillets were easy to apply, whatever the position of the head, and even when the head was too high for the safe application of forceps. They were later superceded entirely by forceps nonetheless.

Forceps/Ventouse – implements to assist natural vaginal delivery that has run into difficulty. Reasons might be when the baby is awkwardly positioned in the birth canal (e.g. shoulder first) or when the woman has become tired due to protracted labour and cannot push sufficiently on her own. A woman is usually given a local anaesthetic before the forceps or Ventouse are inserted. Often an episiotomy (cut) is given to widen the vaginal entrance for these implements. Both methods may leave marks which fade out in a short time. The singer Frank Sinatra famously carried a forcep scar on his face all his life.

Hairnet – as worn by modern medical staff in obstetric and other operating theatres. Not strictly obstetric.

Hoop – here resembling a child's toy which is seen demonstrated by a woman alleged to have been carrying twenty children to help carry the weight of her belly in late pregnancy. It has no name save the one given by Ambroise Paré, the French obstetrician and limb-maker to the French army in the mid-16th century who noticed it in use. He called it – and the lady's condition – 'an admirable thing'.

Incubator gel mattress – gel mattress to line a baby incubator. Transparent blue gel allows xrays through and may be heated to precise temperatures.

Induction – the 'bringing on' of contractions by drug, instrumental or other persuasive means to assist the birthing process. About 10% of babies are delivered using induction before the 37th week of pregnancy. Hormones or drugs used in pessary form can begin this process, allowing contractions – the wave-like muscle spasms of the womb which push the baby into position for birth – to start very fast indeed.

Intra-Uterine Device (IUD) – devices inserted into the cervix in the hope of preventing pregnancy. Pebbles were used in ancient times but the precursor of modern IUDs is generally agreed to be the Gräfenberg Ring, a silver loop which formed the basis of design for most IUD's thereafter. IUDs come in an extraordinary range of shapes and sizes from butterflies to snake bends, coils, curls, anchors and aerials, most usually made in metal, bone or plastic. They are common to almost every culture.

Specula – designed to help obtain a view of the cervix and interior of the womb by holding the vaginal walls apart. Hippocrates was said to have used a speculum in his examinations, though it was not till its development by Joseph Récamier (1774–1852) that the instrument became common again.

Pessary – any device which supports the internal organs of a woman's pelvis when extra support (e.g. due to prolapse or hernia) is needed. They come in a variety of shapes, mostly rings, some solid disks or even inflatable balls and are worn internally.

Sea Tangle Tents – also known as laminaria tents, are extracted from a natural marine plant. Once properly conditioned and sterilized they are used as dilators without pain in the neck of the uterus due to the gradual increase of their size in contact with mucous. This natural plant will keep expanding for 24 hours and increase up to four times their original diameter.

Sponge tampon – a sponge on a silk rope used to prevent pregnancy from occurring by flooding the vagina with spermicidal herbs or other agents.

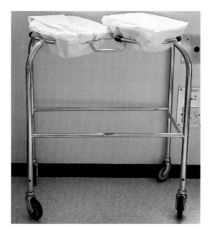

Material	Process
silicon	seal
ink	inscribe
felt	rivet
plaster	dip
clay	pierce
milk	drip
seaweed	thread
pearl	fish
thread	tie
cotton sheet	fold
light	film
salt	pour
bronze	forge
fabric	sew
foam	tear
mother of pearl	engrave
metal	temper
silk	loop
dough	cut
cotton wool	roll
wool	lift
rubber	extrude
porcelain	cast
borosilicate	heat
glass	blow
silver	encapsulate
paper	wrap
sponge	slice
oxygen	filter
stainless steel	roll

Exhibition

Nine light tables
Powder coated steel frame, fluorescent tubes, glass, perspex;
each with a protective perspex cover

loop 1	felt, rivets
loop 2	Jesmonite, felt, rivets
loop 3	silver encapsulated Jesmonite, felt, rivets
dilator	borosilicate glass, foam
imagine 1	DVD player, LCD flat screen monitor
imagine 2	borosilicate glass, text, porcelain
imagine 3	natural sponge, mother of pearl, silk, text
pessary	porcelain
roll	cotton wool

Nine wall panels
Original texts printed on paper

Objects
from the collection of the Hunterian Museum, including:

William Hunter's personal instruments
foetal stethoscope
Michel's suture clips
Hodge pessary
Barne's stem pessary
douche reservoir
vaginal pipe
duck-bill speculum
midwifery forceps with leather covered handles

Acknowledgements

Janice Galloway and Anne Bevan gratefully acknowledge the help of the following organizations and individuals during the making of *Rosengarten,* a project made possible by a Scotish Arts Council Creative Scotland Award to Janice Galloway in 2002.

Sincere thanks are due to the Southern General Hospital, Glasgow; the Royal College of Surgeons, Edinburgh; The Museum of Science and Industry, London; the Hunterian Museum and Art Gallery, Glasgow; the Wellcome Trust, London; the Musée Flaubert et d'Histoire de la Médecine, Rouen; The Museum of Contraception, Toronto; BSJ Electroforming, Middlesex; and Wierside Glass, Sunderland.

Special thanks for their time and patience are due to many individuals, among them David Thomas, Sadie Maskery and Dawn Kemp for their readiness to allow us access to information and archives. The team of Ian Ramsay, Irene Woods and Janice Vandermotten have our especial gratitude for their trust, interest and medical expertise, without which we would not have managed far at all. Thanks also to Mungo Campbell, Donal Bateman, Aileen Nisbet, Maggie Reilly, Chris McClure and Camilla Nicol for their enthusiasm in helping to house and widen the exhibition; to Michael Wolchover for his abiding willingness and splendid work with video and photography; to Norman Veitch, Simon Ward, Andrea Geile and Susan Cross for their know-how and practical application of skills. We are further indebted to Cluny Sheeler of Platform Projects for putting together our book and for his unfailing good humour, calm and house-room.

Final thanks go to Jenny Atallah, Marcel Grant and James. Ta.

Also available:

IRISH (2)
Alec Finlay; photos by Guy Moreton, audio-CD by Zoë Irvine.
Morning Star / Spacex / BALTIC, 2002, ISBN 0 9527669 5 7, £10.00

FOOTBALL MOON
Alec Finlay; type by Jon Harker
Morning Star / BALTIC, 2002, ISBN 0 9527669 4 9, £10.00

COWBOY STORY
Poems by Richard Tuttle, drawings by Heather Deedman, audio CD
by Zoë Irvine; concept by Alec Finlay.
Morning Star / BALTIC, 2002, ISBN 0 9527 669 3 0, £10.00

VERSE CHAIN: SHARING HAIKU & RENGA
Alec Finlay & Martin Lucas
Morning Star / BALTIC 2003, ISBN 1 904477 01 1, £10.00

WIND BLOWN CLOUD
Alec Finlay
Morning Star / BALTIC 2003, ISBN 1 904477 03 8, £10.00

FRIDAY 8 MAY
Alexander & Susan Maris.
platform / Morning Star / BALTIC, 2003, ISBN 1 904477 04 6, £10.00

BYNAMES
an anthology of invented bynames, Epic Filly
platform / Morning Star / BALTIC, 2003, ISBN 1 904477 02 X, £10.00

A platform projects book
Designed by Cluny Sheeler and Lucy Richards
Printed by Scotprint, Haddington, East Lothian

Edition of 1,500 copies

Published by:
Platform Projects
21A West Mayfield
Edinburgh, EH9 1TQ

Hunterian Art Gallery
University of Glasgow
82 Hillhead Street
Glasgow, G12 8QQ

UNIVERSITY
of
GLASGOW

'TABLE XXXV', from H. F. Kilian's *Geburtschüflicher Atlas*, 1835, reproduced by permission of the Wellcome Library, London

Anne Bevan's research was supported by Edinburgh College of Art and the Arts and Humanities Research Board

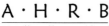

A · H · R · B
arts and humanities research board

The publishers acknowledge support from the Scottish Arts Council towards the publication of this title.

Scottish
Arts Council
LOTTERY FUNDED

ISBN 0 9546831 0 2